GODS AND GODDESSES
OF
ANCIENT
EGYPT

LEON ASHWORTH

SMART APPLE MEDIA

First published by Cherrytree Books
(a member of the Evans Publishing Group)
2A Portman Mansions, Chiltern Street
London W1U 6NR, United Kingdom
Copyright © Evans Brothers Limited 2001
This edition published under license from
Evans Brothers Limited.
All rights reserved.

Text by Leon Ashworth
Cover design by The Design Lab

Published in the United States by
Smart Apple Media
1980 Lookout Drive
North Mankato, MN 56003

ISBN 1-58340-196-2

Library of Congress Control Number: 2002 141258

2 4 6 8 9 7 5 3 1

Acknowledgments
Design: Richard Rowan
Artwork: Gwen Green
Consultant: Peter A Clayton FSA
Photographs by: AKG London, 1, 2 left top (& spine) & bottom, 3 bottom
(& cover), 4 top & bottom, 6 left, 6/7, 8/9, 9 top & center & cover, 10
bottom left, 10/11, 12 bottom, 14 bottom left & right, 15, 16 bottom left, 17
top left & bottom, 19 bottom, 21 bottom left (& back cover) & right, 24
bottom right, 25, 26 (& cover), 27 right top, center & bottom left, 28, 28/29,
29 top right & bottom left; Peter Clayton, 2 right, 3 top, 4 center, 5, 6 top, 7
top left & right, 9 bottom right, 10 bottom right, 11, 12 top left, 13, 14 top,
14/15, 16 top right, 17 top right, 18, 20, 20/21, 22, 23, 24 top right & bottom
left, 27 bottom right, 29 left center & bottom right

CONTENTS

ANCIENT EGYPT	4
PHARAOHS, PRIESTS, AND PEOPLE	6
TEMPLES AND FESTIVALS	8
RE, THE SUN GOD	10
NUT AND GEB	12
OSIRIS, GOD OF AGRICULTURE	14
ISIS, GODDESS OF NATURE	16
SETH AND HORUS	18
HATHOR, THE COW GODDESS	20
ANUBIS, GOD OF DEATH	22
THOTH, GOD OF WISDOM	24
AMON AND ATON	26
ANIMALS AS GODS	28
GLOSSARY	30
INDEX	32

ANCIENT EGYPT

EGYPT IS A LAND in one of the hottest, driest parts of Africa. The first people to live in this region were nomads who wandered the desert hunting wild animals and herding sheep and goats. The gods these people worshipped took the form of local animals, such as birds and crocodiles and hippos.

Most of Egypt is desert, but on either side of the river Nile the land is green. It was made fertile by flooding that occurred every year. In this rich land, people settled and started to grow crops. The farmers built villages and towns, and in them temples for their gods. Some of the gods took human shape but still kept an animal's head, horns, ears, or beak. Each place had its own god.

FAMILY OF GODS

When villages joined together to make a town or city, each wanted to keep its own god. So the gods had to get together too. Some became a family of gods—mother, father, and children. Others had their names—and stories—merged to make one. In this way Ancient Egypt came to have many gods. Their stories varied from place to place and from age to age. This book describes the stories of the most important gods.

▲ The Egyptians became farmers and used animals to help with farm work. They worshipped many gods that took the form of animals, including bulls.

BIRTH OF THE GODS

Before the world began, there was watery darkness called Nun—an ocean that contained the seeds of all things inside a spirit called Atum. A muddy hill rose from the waters, and with it, the creator god. Having created himself, this god then coughed from his mouth Shu (air) and Tefnut (moisture). Shu parted the earth (Geb) from the sky (Nut), who then gave birth to five children: Osiris, Horus, Isis, Seth, and Nephthys. From the ocean too, people believed, the mighty river Nile (below) had sprung.

▲ The Egyptians held many animals sacred and often mummified their bodies when they died (see page 28). This is the mummy of a sacred cat.

◄ The Egyptians carved images of their gods and goddesses in stone and wrote about them in picture-writing called hieroglyphics.

◄ Many tourists visit Egypt to see its historic remains. Here tourist boats are moored alongside an ancient temple.

FAMILY OF THE EGYPTIAN GODS

ATUM (RE)
creator god and sun god

AMON
god of Thebes who became Egypt's chief god

ATON
god who took Amon's place for a short time

HATHOR
cow goddess and daughter of Re

TEFNUT = **SHU**
goddess of moisture, twin of Shu / god of air, twin of Tefnut

NUT = **GEB**
goddess of the sky, twin of Geb / god of the earth, twin of Nut

THOTH
god of wisdom and inventor of picture-writing

HORUS
the elder, falcon-headed sky god

ISIS = **OSIRIS**
nature goddess, sister and wife of Osiris / god of agriculture and the underworld, brother and husband of Isis

NEPHTHYS = **SETH**
sister and wife of Seth, mother of Anubis / god of the desert and darkness, brother and husband of Nephthys

HORUS
son of Isis and Osiris, nephew of Seth

ANUBIS
jackal-headed god of death and funerals, son of Nephthys

▲ The most important family of gods was headed by Atum. Later, Re, or Ra, joined the family and merged with Atum, and with Amon.

= MARRIAGE

PHARAOHS, PRIESTS, AND PEOPLE

THE EGYPTIANS saw the world of the gods as part of the earthly world in which they lived, and the world they would dwell in after death. Both gods and people were ruled by the king, or pharaoh, whose task was to keep the world in order. This order, or balance, was called ma'at, and in time Ma'at became a goddess of law, truth, and justice. The heart of every dead person was weighed against Ma'at, to test its truthfulness.

LAW AND ORDER

As well as heading the army, navy, law courts, and state religion, the king owned all the land, property, and even people. Under him were the nobles. Next came government officials, civil servants, and other educated people such as teachers, doctors, lawyers, mathematicians, astronomers, architects, scribes (writers of documents), and priests.

Most priests worked part-time, serving in the temple for three months before returning to their jobs as doctors or lawyers. Craftsmen included stonemasons, jewelers, and smiths, who worked for wealthy families and temples. Most ordinary people were craftworkers, builders, and farmers. Many were slaves.

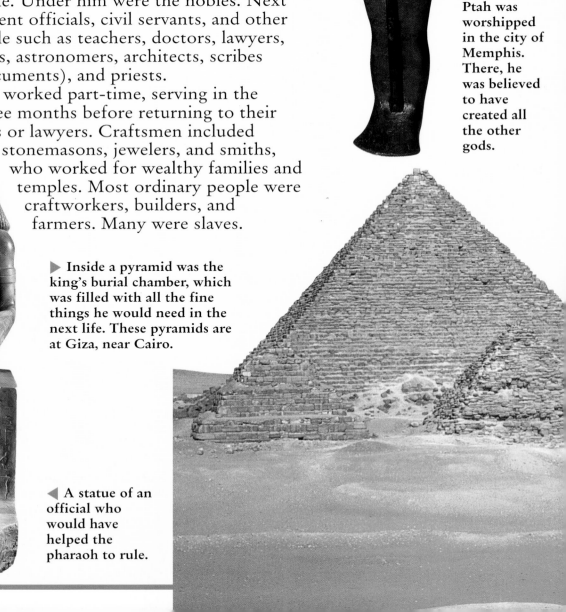

◀ The god Ptah was worshipped in the city of Memphis. There, he was believed to have created all the other gods.

▶ Inside a pyramid was the king's burial chamber, which was filled with all the fine things he would need in the next life. These pyramids are at Giza, near Cairo.

◀ A statue of an official who would have helped the pharaoh to rule.

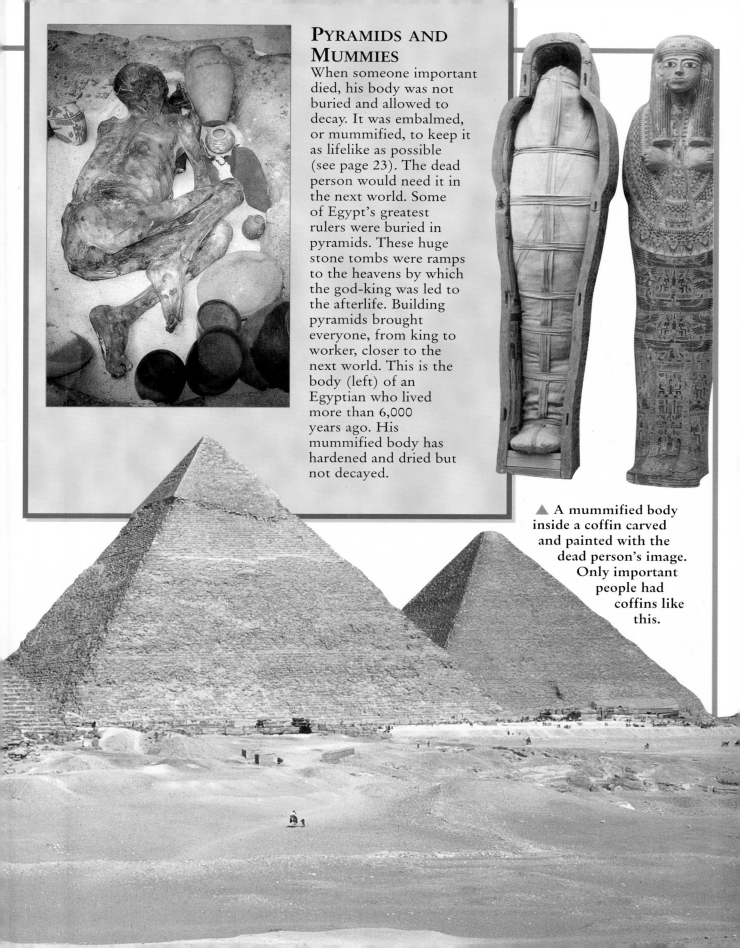

PYRAMIDS AND MUMMIES

When someone important died, his body was not buried and allowed to decay. It was embalmed, or mummified, to keep it as lifelike as possible (see page 23). The dead person would need it in the next world. Some of Egypt's greatest rulers were buried in pyramids. These huge stone tombs were ramps to the heavens by which the god-king was led to the afterlife. Building pyramids brought everyone, from king to worker, closer to the next world. This is the body (left) of an Egyptian who lived more than 6,000 years ago. His mummified body has hardened and dried but not decayed.

▲ A mummified body inside a coffin carved and painted with the dead person's image. Only important people had coffins like this.

Temples and Festivals

A T THE HEART of an Egyptian temple was a sacred chamber, a shrine where the god lived, usually in the form of a statue or an animal. Only the king—the god's son—had the right to stand in the holy presence. But the king could not attend to the god all the time, so he gave this right to his high priest.

Large temples had four main priests, with many others to perform rituals and offer the prayers that people asked for. All priests were men, but women could be temple dancers and singers. They sang to wake the god up every morning.

FESTIVALS

Ordinary Egyptians played no part in the temple rituals. They prayed at home and saw the god only at festival times, when the statue

▼ The Egyptians were fine builders. They built palaces for their kings and temples for their gods. This is the temple of Horus at Edfu.

IN THE TEMPLE

The priests cared for the god's every want. Each day they opened the shrine to clean the statue. They dressed it in fresh clothes, makeup, and jewelry, and then placed food and drink before it. Later they took the meal away, to eat as payment for their work. Meals were offered again at midday and in the evening, before the statue was made ready for the night. In return, the god watched over his people, keeping their crops and animals healthy. Any god who was not served well might send plagues, famines, or other disasters.

was taken out in procession. Festivals meant feasting, sacrifices, and carnival. Some lasted several days, with music, dancing, singing, eating, and drinking. The most popular were dedicated to Osiris, Amon-Re, Horus, and Hathor.

▲ The Egyptians invented many musical instruments, which were played by women at festivals and in the temple.

▼ This wall painting shows a priest wearing a leopard skin to show his high rank.

DRINKING TO THE GODS

Festivals at the elegant temple of Bast (see page 28), the cat goddess (above), were very popular. Hundreds of thousands of visitors flocked to Bubastis for the annual fair, journeying by barge to the sound of flutes and castanets. Women watching from the riverside joked and called to the pilgrims as they passed by. On the festival day, when the procession wound around the town, more wine was drunk than in the whole remainder of the year.

RE, THE SUN GOD

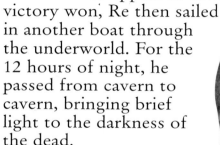

THE RIVER NILE gave Egypt life. But in that desert land the fierce, burning sun was an even stronger force. The sun god was the official god of Egypt's rulers. Every king called himself the son of Re and was regarded as the sun god in human form.

BATTLING AGAINST DARKNESS

The story of Re explained the daily appearance and disappearance of the sun. Re was light. Every day he sailed his fiery gold ship across the sky, shedding warmth on the earth. But at journey's end in the west lay his terrible enemy, the serpent Apophis, eager to devour him and cast the world into darkness. Each night Re and his servants battled with the dreaded enemy, so that, as the sun, he would live to appear at dawn. The victory won, Re then sailed in another boat through the underworld. For the 12 hours of night, he passed from cavern to cavern, bringing brief light to the darkness of the dead.

▲ A woman worships Re, with his falcon's head, and feels the benefit of his light.

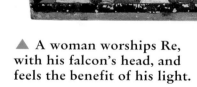

▲ The sun was shown as Re at noon and Atum at night. At dawn it was Khephri, a sacred beetle. Khephri moved the sun across the sky in the way a scarab rolls a ball of dung along. This scarab is part of a jewel.

◄ Re carries on his head the sun surrounded by the serpent Apophis. Behind him is Atum.

Helping with Spells

Every day the priests prayed for the defeat of Apophis. In the temple at Thebes they performed a daily ritual to help Re. They made a wax figure of the serpent and inscribed his name on it in green ink. Then they attacked the model. They insulted it, stabbed it with a knife, and hurled it to the ground. All the while the priests recited a spell. If all went well, Re would scatter his enemies, and the sun would break through the darkness the next day. In this picture, a cat is slaying the serpent.

Sacred Boat

Re traveled through the sky and the underworld in a sacred boat such as this one carrying a party of gods. Boats were important to the Egyptians because they lived on a river. The pyramid was both a staircase to the sky and a jetty from which a spirit boat could sail. A 5,000-year-old boat found in a pit near the Great Pyramid at Giza may have been intended for the dead king's voyage.

NUT AND GEB

THE EGYPTIANS watched the sky by day and by night. The stories of Nut and Geb explained the movements of the heavenly bodies and the split between earth and sky. The sky itself was the goddess Nut, daughter of Shu (air) and his sister-wife Tefnut (moisture).

Nut's own twin brother was the earth god Geb. Some said that Nut and Geb were born locked in each other's arms. Others, that the two married in secret and angered their grandfather, Re. Whatever happened, Re ordered Shu to separate the pair. The air god tried with all his might to tear them apart, but Nut held fast to Geb with her fingers and toes. Her body arched over him, forming the sky.

GEB AND THE SERPENT

Geb was curious to know the contents of a magic box that Re had placed in a fortress along with a lock of his hair. Recklessly, Geb ordered the box to be opened. Inside was the uraeus, a terrifying, flame-spitting serpent. The flames burned Geb so badly that only Re could save him, for Re could heal as well as destroy. When the lock of Re's hair was placed on his wound, Geb was made well again. The kings who followed Geb carried on their forehead an emblem of the uraeus, the symbol of Re's—and the sun's—blistering power.

SKY WATCHING

Being farmers, the Egyptians needed to know when to plant and harvest their crops, and when the Nile would flood. Their astronomers studied the night sky and noticed that Sirius, the Dog Star, disappeared for 70 days (when

 Like earthly kings of Egypt, Geb married his sister. As gods themselves, the pharaohs could not usually marry a person of non-royal birth.

▶ The goddess Nut stretches her arms and wings over the earth. She was often painted on coffin lids because she was the mother of Osiris, god of the underworld.

CHILDREN OF MOONLIGHT

The angry Re punished Nut. No children could be born to her on any day of the year, he ordered. But a clever god called Thoth (see page 24) took pity on her. He challenged the moon to gamble part of its light in a game of checkers. With the light he won he made five extra days. On these days Nut gave birth to her children: Osiris, Horus (the elder), Seth, Isis, and Nephthys. As for the moon, it can be seen losing its light, little by little, every month. In this way the Egyptians explained the phases of the moon.

ANCESTOR OF THE PHARAOHS

Geb followed his father Shu as ruler of the world. The old air god was overthrown by a revolt of his followers. For nine days, a terrible tempest shook the world. Then Shu fled to the skies, and Geb took his throne.

The new ruler drew up a report on every town and province in Egypt. He proved so wise a ruler that the earthly kings claimed him as their ancestor, and their royal throne was called the throne of Geb. When Geb also grew old, he handed power over to his eldest son, Osiris.

its brightness was eclipsed by the sun) each year. It reappeared just as the annual flood began.

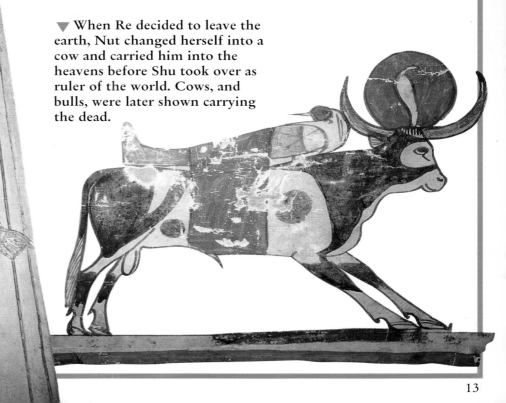

▼ When Re decided to leave the earth, Nut changed herself into a cow and carried him into the heavens before Shu took over as ruler of the world. Cows, and bulls, were later shown carrying the dead.

OSIRIS, GOD OF AGRICULTURE

OSIRIS WAS the first child of Nut and Geb. After Geb left the earth for heaven, Osiris took the throne of Egypt and married Isis, his sister. Osiris was handsome, dark-skinned, and taller than all other men. He was the fourth god to rule the earth, and earned the name the Good One.

Osiris brought civilization to Egypt. He taught people how to grow grain and grapes, how to make farm tools, and how to make bread, beer, and wine. He taught them how to worship, build temples, and carve images of the gods. He built towns and made just laws. He even invented the flute to accompany the singing at religious ceremonies.

OSIRIS MURDERED

The god Seth was so jealous of his brother that he plotted to kill him and become king. He invited Osiris to a party, and when all the guests were enjoying themselves, a large, carved chest was carried into the room. Everyone admired it. "Why not try it for size?" suggested Seth. Anyone who fitted it exactly could have it, he said. So each guest stepped inside and laid down, but all found it too big. Then Osiris, taller than all other men, laid down inside the chest. Yes, it was just the right size—for a coffin. Seth's men banged down the lid, sealed it, and threw it into the Nile. The chest floated away.

▶ **This is part of a statue of Osiris from the temple of Abu Simbel.**

◀ **In this wall painting, Osiris wears the pharaoh's crown. He carries a flail for threshing corn, and a shepherd's crook.**

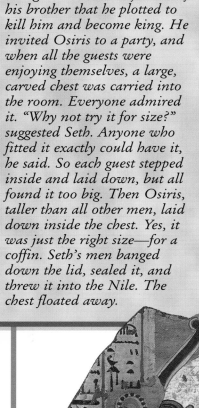

Osiris had over 100 names and titles, and many shapes. Here he is seen as the bird Bennu, which was believed to rise from the dead.

Harvest Time

The Egyptians had Osiris to thank for the good things of life, their daily bread and the beer and wine that went with it. Because of the flooding of the Nile, the soil of Egypt was rich. As soon as the floodwaters subsided in October, farmers plowed their fields and sowed their seeds of wheat or barley. Harvest time was in March or April.

Traveler and Treachery

One day Osiris left his home to spread the skills of civilization to the rest of the world. Leaving his wife Isis to rule Egypt, he went to Asia, which he won over by music and gentleness. Osiris hated violence. He traveled the world, spreading civilization wherever he went.

But Osiris had enemies, including his jealous brother Seth, who plotted against him and brought about his death. After dying, Osiris was given the chance to return to life by the loyal Isis. Instead, the god chose to leave the earth and reign in the world of the dead.

God of the Dead

As god of the dead, Osiris was worshipped throughout Egypt and rivaled Re as the foremost god. At death, the king of Egypt became Osiris.

In this cloth painting, Osiris and the jackal-headed god Anubis escort a dead person to the underworld.

ISIS, GODDESS OF NATURE

ISIS WAS the first daughter of Nut and Geb. As wife of her brother Osiris and mother of their child Horus, she became the most popular goddess of ancient Egypt. People told how Isis taught women to grind grain and make flour; how to spin and weave cloth; how to nurse the sick. Everything to do with marriage was in her care. Isis the great enchantress wove magic charms and spells. People called on her in illness, for had she not restored her husband to life?

▶ This wooden statuette shows Isis kneeling. On her head is the throne of Egypt, which is the hieroglyph of her name.

FINDING RE'S NAME

Isis was determined to gain Re's power. To do so she had to discover the secret name of Re, known only to himself. Re was by now a feeble, dribbling old man. Isis mixed some of his spittle into the earth to make a poisonous snake, which she left in the god's path. Sure enough, the snake bit Re. Poison spread through his body and he begged Isis to save him with her healing skills. To be cured, Isis told him, he must speak his secret name. Re tried many false names, but the poison gripped him in such agony that at last the god was forced to reveal his true name. Isis gained Re's secret and, with it, his great power.

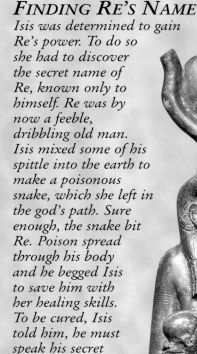

◀ Isis, the best-loved goddess of Egypt, and her son Horus. On her head she wears the disc of the sun between a cow's horns.

SEARCH FOR OSIRIS

At news of Osiris's murder, Isis wept. She tore her clothes to ribbons and cut off her long, dark hair. Then she vowed to find her husband.

The wooden chest in which Osiris lay floated to a faraway shore. It landed at the foot of a tree, which in time grew around it. One day, the tree was cut down by order of the local ruler, who was building a palace.

HOME LIFE

The women of Egypt ran the home, brought up the children, and performed all kinds of domestic duties. A wife also had many rights and, like the goddess Isis, ran her husband's affairs when he was away. Families in Egypt were

▲ This painted clay statuette is of a woman at a mixing tub making beer.

A wondrous fragrance filled the air, so marvelous that news of it spread far and wide. Isis felt that the wonder was linked to Osiris. She asked for the tree trunk to be split open—and inside found the chest.

Isis took the chest home to Egypt and opened it. Then she turned herself into a hawk and with beating wings tried to fan life back into the dead Osiris. Again using magic, she became pregnant. Then she hid herself in the marshes by the river. There, while out hunting by moonlight, Seth discovered the chest and the body inside it.

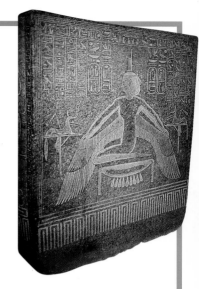

▲ The winged figure of Isis adorns the end of this sarcophagus (stone coffin). Isis was the chief mourner for her husband and was important in all funeral rites.

▼ Isis, crowned with the disc of the sun between the horns of a cow, stands beside her husband, who crouches on the pedestal next to his son Horus.

much like our own. Women had almost as many rights as men. They could own a house, inherit land from a relative, buy and sell goods, and divorce a husband. Few women went to school—they learned domestic skills such as sewing and weaving at home.

17

SETH AND HORUS

SETH WAS the son of Geb and Nut. He married his sister Nephthys and reigned over the desert. He was a deadly rival to his brother Osiris, whose kingdom covered the fertile lands. After killing Osiris, who was just and good, Seth took his place as ruler. To escape his cruelty, Isis fled into hiding. She had only seven scorpions for company—until her son Horus was born.

She had hidden her husband's body, but Seth found it and destroyed it, as he thought, forever. But Isis was too clever for him and restored her husband's life (see panel).

SAVING OSIRIS

When Seth found Osiris's body hidden in the marshes, he hacked it to bits and scattered the pieces far and wide. Piece by piece, Isis tracked down her husband's remains—all but one that a Nile fish had eaten. Skillfully, she fitted the pieces back together on the river bank. Then she washed them with oils, and Anubis (see page 22) wrapped them in bandages. This, the first-ever rite of embalming the dead, gave to Osiris eternal life. But Osiris chose to leave the land of the living and rule over the dead in the underworld.

▲ As a boy, Horus was surrounded by dangers: snakes, scorpions, and crocodiles, all of which were associated with Seth.

▼ Seth is often shown as a mythical beast with a jackal-like body and snout and alert, square-topped ears.

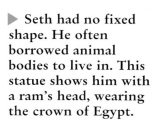

▶ Seth had no fixed shape. He often borrowed animal bodies to live in. This statue shows him with a ram's head, wearing the crown of Egypt.

▲ A statue of Horus in the shape of a falcon. His mother had changed into a bird when her son was conceived, so he is often shown as a bird too.

FEAR OF THE DESERT

The Egyptians feared the desert, though they admired its strength. They called on Seth when their armies went to war. Seth was wild and rough like a desert storm. When they were not at war, people hated Seth and loved his courageous nephew, Isis's son Horus.

HORUS CHALLENGES SETH

To escape Seth's anger, Isis again hid with Horus in the marshes. The boy god had been weak at birth. Among many dangers, he faced being bitten by savage beasts, burnt by the sun, and stung by scorpions. Only his mother's magic saved him. Osiris often returned to earth to visit the boy, preparing him for the fight with Seth that would avenge his death. So Horus grew to manhood and claimed his right to rule before the court of the gods. When he came to be judged, Seth put every obstacle in his way, but eventually the gods granted Horus the throne.

◄ Horus was a link with his father in the underworld and often guided the dead to judgment before the throne of Osiris.

HATHOR, THE COW GODDESS

THE EGYPTIANS liked to enjoy themselves, and the cow goddess Hathor gave them a good excuse. She was goddess of joy, beauty, love, and marriage. She helped mothers and babies in childbirth, and young women with their clothes and makeup. Great festivals were held at her temple, especially on her birthday, which was New Year's Day.

Before dawn, priests took her image out onto the terrace to face the rays of the rising sun. Then came the celebrations, with parties, music, singing, and dancing. The goddess carried a musical instrument—a jingling rattle called a sistrum—to drive away evil spirits with its noise.

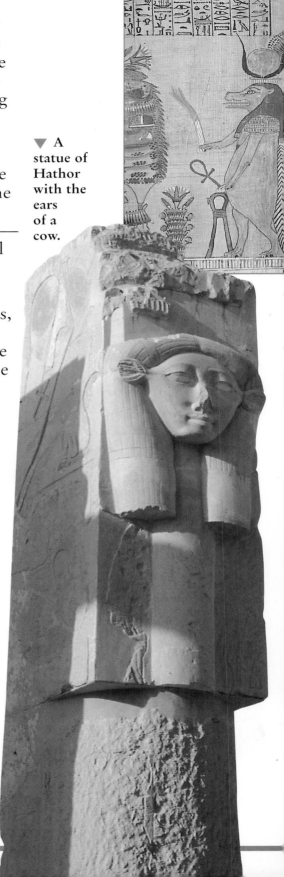

▼ A statue of Hathor with the ears of a cow.

FEEDING THE GODS
When Isis gave birth to Horus, Re sent Shu and Thoth to bring Hathor to Egypt. Her milk fed the infant Horus (below), and she later married him. Then her milk became the food of the gods. At first she lived with them in heaven, entertaining them with singing and dancing. Then, when Seth attacked Horus in a duel, she saved Horus's eyesight. Seth tried to make off with her to his palace of darkness, but Horus came to her rescue and gave her a new home at Dendera, where her main temple was.

FOOD FOR THE GODS
Hathor was a sky goddess, the daughter of Re. But she was also known as the great cow who created the world and everything in it, including the sun. In her, the sun god lived at night, ready to be born each morning. She is often shown as a cow or with a cow's head. But usually she has a human head with horns or cow's ears.

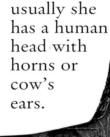

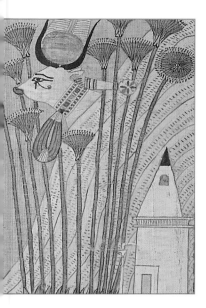

GODDESS OF THE DRESSING TABLE

The wealthy of Egypt took great trouble over their appearance. Both women and men wore makeup. Red lip powder and painted nails were popular. People painted their eyebrows grey, black, or green, and gave their eyes dark outlines. Women wore their hair cut straight to the shoulder or longer down the back. Both men and women wore wigs, perhaps to protect them from the sun. For formal occasions, wealthy women wore a headdress. On top was a scented cone of wax that slowly melted, releasing a sweet smell. Cosmetics and jewelry were left with the dead for use in the afterlife.

▲ Hathor was important to the dead. Sometimes she hid in a tree on the edge of the desert near where the dead were buried. She gave them welcome bread and water.

▼ Another god who protected women was the cheerful little god of the home, Bes. He watched over women in childbirth and kept the family safe from evil spirits, snakes, scorpions, and other harmful creatures.

▼ Music was important to the Egyptians. Here a harpist plays for a wealthy couple. The harp was accompanied by Hathor's instrument, the sistrum.

ANUBIS, GOD OF DEATH

ANUBIS, SON of Osiris and Nephthys, was god of death and decay. Because jackals scavenged around burial places, people associated them with the dead. So Anubis was part-jackal in shape.

SAVING THE BODY

Young Anubis had been left by his mother. He was found and brought up by his aunt, Isis, and then set out with Osiris to conquer the world. Later, by helping to bind and bury Osiris's body, he became known as "Lord of the Mummy Wrappings." He was credited with inventing the Egyptian process of mummification.

When people died in Egypt, families placed their trust in Anubis. He presided over the funeral rites and guarded the person's tomb. While the dead person's body was being embalmed, the priests in charge wore a jackal mask to show that the god was present.

JUDGMENT OF OSIRIS

A dead person faced Osiris and his judges. Before them stood the scales of judgment in which Anubis placed the dead person's heart, to weigh against the feather of truth. Would the scales balance? Had the owner led a good life or caused harm? Thoth, the record-keeper (see page 24), wrote down the result. Those who passed the test looked forward to paradise. Those who failed fell prey to Ammit the Gobbler—part-crocodile, part-lion, and part-hippopotamus—lying in wait to devour them.

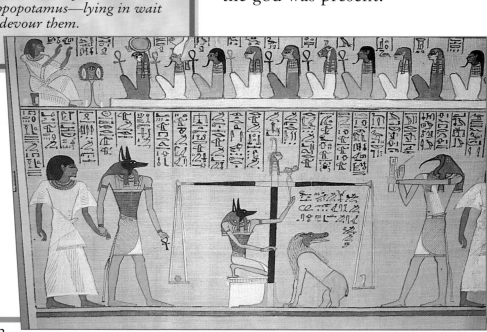

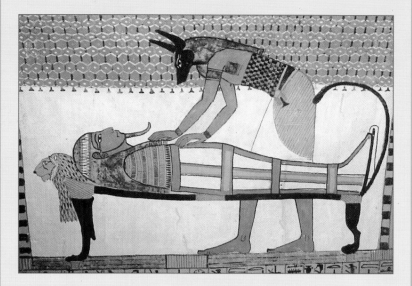

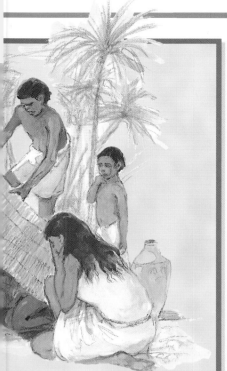

BURYING THE DEAD

The poorest people could not afford mummification. They were simply buried in the desert sand. Richer people had coffins, usually wooden and decorated. Important people such as the king had a series of coffins, each fitting inside the other. The innermost were usually shaped like a person, with a face painted on top. On the day of the funeral, the coffin was carried to the tomb on a sleigh, followed by priests, relatives, friends, and perhaps hired mourners to lead the lamenting. They carried food, furniture, prized possessions, models of servants—all to be buried with the mummy for use in the afterlife.

◀ Anubis protected graves from robbers and was often shown as a dog on guard.

MUMMY-MAKING

Making a mummy took 70 days. First the embalmers made a cut on the left side of the body. They took out the soft insides and stored them in pots called canopic jars (below). They left the person's heart in place but drew out the brains through the nostrils. They rubbed the body with salt-like natron crystals to dry it. Then they washed it and smeared it with pine resin, which would set hard and protect the flesh. They packed the inside with wads of linen, also soaked in resin. Then they wrapped it in as many as 20 layers of cloth.

Anubis also greeted the dead person, now a mummy, at the door of the tomb and made sure that offerings from the family reached the dead person. He opened the roads of the other world for the dead to travel. Then, taking them by the hand, he brought them before Osiris for judgment and the weighing of their souls.

THOTH, GOD OF WISDOM

THE FIRST people to write anything more than records were probably the Egyptians. They used their picture-writing for recording knowledge, writing down stories and poems, inscribing monuments, and for everyday letters. The god they thanked for their wisdom and skills was the moon god Thoth. He had invented writing along with all other branches of knowledge, including astronomy, art, mathematics, science, law, magic, medicine, and music. Thoth was the patron of scribes and doctors. Sometimes he was said to have created the

RULER OF TIME

Thoth's magic helped restore Osiris when Isis bound up his body. Later the god protected Isis and Horus in hiding and saved the child from a scorpion sting. He healed the wounded Horus during his wars with Seth and finally judged in the young god's favor at the court of the gods.

Thoth followed Horus as ruler on earth and reigned for 3,226 years. Then he left for the sky and became the moon god. He joined Re in his boat, taking the sun god's place in the night sky while Re traveled to the underworld.

One of Thoth's tasks was to measure time, dividing it into months, years, and the three Egyptian seasons.

▲ Sometimes Thoth is shown as a baboon or baboon-headed man.

▼ As inventor of hieroglyphs, Thoth was called "Lord of Holy Words."

▼ Thoth is usually shown with an ibis head. Here he is at work in the underworld, recording the judgment of souls. Behind him is Ammit the Gobbler.

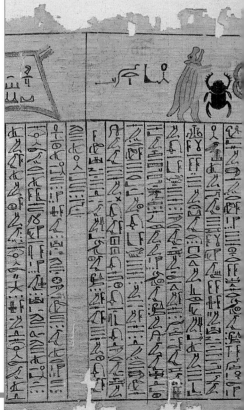

BECOMING A SCRIBE

Learning to write hieroglyphs was difficult. Children practiced on limestone slabs using reed pens dipped in ink made of soot dissolved in gum and water. Boys aged from 4 to 16 studied to be scribes. They had to learn hundreds of characters; there were at least 20 different signs for "bird." A qualified scribe would keep written records and might write letters for fellow villagers. If he rose to high office, he might serve the pharaoh himself.

world, by naming it after rising from the ocean of Nun. In the underworld, Thoth recorded the weighing of the hearts of the dead. He was the vizier (counselor) of Osiris and the sacred scribe of his kingdom.

MATH AND MAGIC

The Egyptians used the phases of the moon as a way of counting. Thoth, the moon god, became god of reckoning and then of learning in general. He was the creator of language, interpreter and advisor of the gods, and the representative of the sun god Re on earth.

Because he possessed some of Re's universal knowledge, Thoth understood time and truth. Some stories say his knowledge came from books in his father's library, which only he knew how to read. By studying the books, Thoth learned the arts of magic. It was said that Thoth's magic books were owned by his priests and held the secrets of the universe.

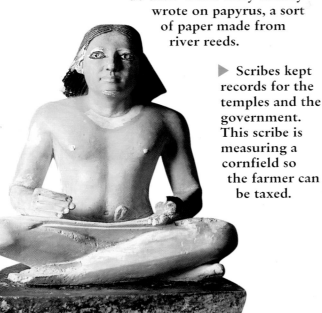

▼ Scribes sat cross-legged to do their work. They usually wrote on papyrus, a sort of paper made from river reeds.

▶ Scribes kept records for the temples and the government. This scribe is measuring a cornfield so the farmer can be taxed.

AMON AND ATON

AMON WAS a god of the air, born from the voice of Thoth. His name meant "secret god," and he protected the area around Thebes (modern Luxor), where he was worshipped as a curly-horned ram. When Thebes was capital of Egypt (around 1550 to 1070 B.C.), he became the most important god in the country. His priests at Thebes and Karnak claimed him as a form of the sun god Re and began calling him Amon-Re. Under this name, he became Egypt's national god. His name was added to the king's official titles, and for 2,000 years he reigned supreme as father and ruler of all gods in Egypt.

ATON—THE ONE AND ONLY SUN GOD

Amon's rule was broken for a time by the pharaoh Amenhotep, who reigned around 1360 B.C. This king had his own ideas about religion. He worshipped a god called the Aton—and made everyone else do the same. Aton became the only god allowed in all of Egypt.

Aton was the sun disc, the body of Re. Until now he had been just one of Re's forms—and not very important. Now he reigned alone. The king changed his own name to Akhenaton ("he who pleases Aton"). He moved the capital from

▶ Amon was often shown with the head—and strength—of a ram.

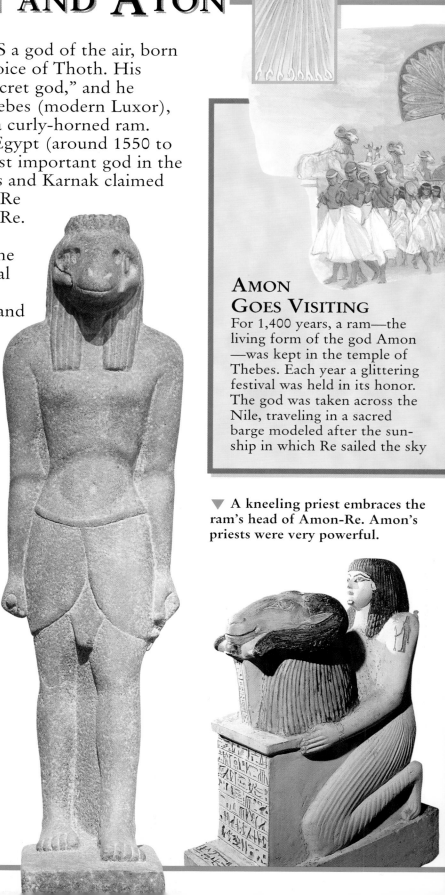

AMON GOES VISITING

For 1,400 years, a ram—the living form of the god Amon—was kept in the temple of Thebes. Each year a glittering festival was held in its honor. The god was taken across the Nile, traveling in a sacred barge modeled after the sun-ship in which Re sailed the sky

▼ A kneeling priest embraces the ram's head of Amon-Re. Amon's priests were very powerful.

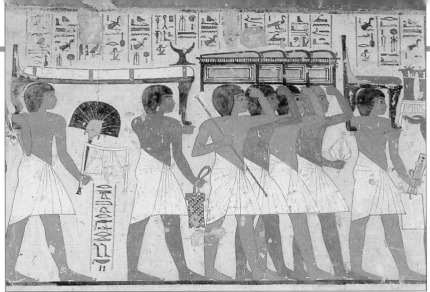

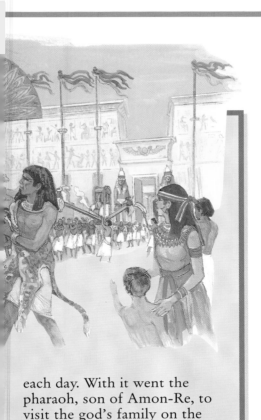

each day. With it went the pharaoh, son of Amon-Re, to visit the god's family on the far bank of the Nile, in what was to become the Valley of the Kings.

Thebes (Amon's city) to a newly built city called Akhetaton (Amarna). Here, with his wife Nefertiti and six daughters, the king worshipped Aton. The priests of Amon were furious. When a new king came to the throne, they talked him into restoring Amon as chief god. The young king added Amon's name to his—and he became Tutankhamon.

▲ This wall painting shows servants carrying the furnishings for the tomb of a high official. Funeral processions were elaborate and important events.

▶ Tutankhamon died at about the age of 18. The head of his mummy was covered with this magnificent gold mask.

▼ Amon's temple at Karnak near Thebes was the greatest in all of Egypt. But Akhenaton abandoned it to build a new center of worship for the Aton.

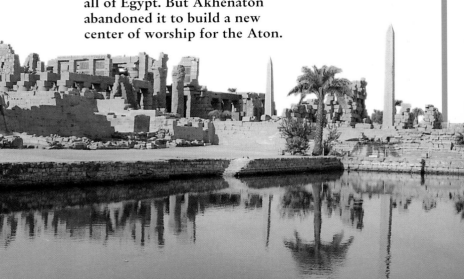

▲ The Aton was shown as the disc of the sun, with rays that ended in human hands. Here he is being worshipped by the pharaoh Akhenaton.

ANIMALS AS GODS

I N EARLY TIMES, Egyptians chose an animal as their local mascot. Hawks and falcons were popular because of their speed and the way they swooped out of the sun onto their prey. Snakes and crocodiles were chosen because they could harm people and so scare away enemies. Dogs, cats, and geese were loyal friends who could sound an alarm when danger threatened.

SACRED BUT SACRIFICED

Egyptians did not normally worship animals. They kept some as pets and used some as a way of making offerings to the gods. In most temples, the local god or goddess was supposed to be present in the animal kept in the sanctuary—a cat in the temple of Bast, a falcon or ibis in the temple of Horus or Thoth. Later, every single animal of the same type came to be seen as sacred. They could be sacrificed to the god, but it was forbidden to kill or eat them. Cats, hawks, and ibis were venerated all over Egypt. To kill them, even accidentally, was to risk death from an angry mob.

CATS BRING LUCK

In the city of Bubastis, cats representing the goddess Bast were specially honored. Bast had been made

SACRED BULLS

From early times, kings of Egypt were linked with the bull. As kings became gods, so did bulls. The god Ptah was supposed to be reborn in the sacred Apis bull of Memphis,

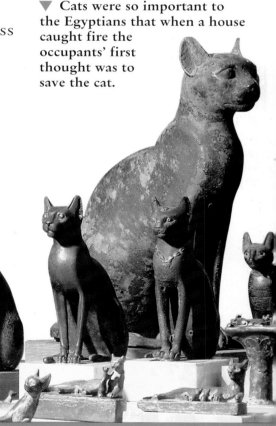

▼ Cats were so important to the Egyptians that when a house caught fire the occupants' first thought was to save the cat.

28

so angry by her father, Re, that she turned herself into a lion. Later, as she bathed in the river, her anger cooled and she became a domestic cat. Her cat servants brought good luck to people's homes, and parents hung her picture around children's necks as a lucky charm. Thousands of people went to the yearly festival at her temple (see page 9).

SACRED CROCODILES

Crocodilopolis was the home of Sobek, a crocodile god that lived in a lake dug near the great temple.

The old crocodile had golden rings in its ears and bracelets on its forelegs. Visitors enjoyed watching the animal and its family being fed. One tourist reported: "Priests approached it, and while one of them held open its jaws, another put in the cake and the meat and poured in the honey-wine."

which lived in its own temple opposite the god's. Each day it was let out into the courtyard, where tourists flocked to see it. Another bull called Mnevis, at Hermopolis, was sacred to Atum-Re.

▶ The ibis was associated with the god Thoth.

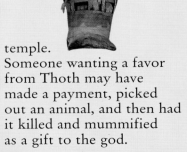

MUMMIFIED PETS

Egyptians often mummified dead animals. Archaeologists have found not only hundreds of thousands of cats (right), but also mice and rats (food for the cat on its journey to the underworld), all kinds of birds, lizards, crocodiles, dogs, gazelles, and rams. A cemetery dedicated to Thoth was found crammed with mummified baboons and ibis (left)— well over four million ibis mummies alone.

The animals may have been kept and reared in a compound near the temple. Someone wanting a favor from Thoth may have made a payment, picked out an animal, and then had it killed and mummified as a gift to the god.

GLOSSARY

archaeologist Person who studies the remains of ancient civilizations.

architect Person who designs buildings and other structures.

astronomer Person who studies the stars and planets.

barge Small sailing boat once used on rivers; modern barges are large and motor-driven.

canopic jar Vase, with a lid shaped like a human or animal head, used for storing the internal organs of the dead.

carnival Time of merry-making, parades, and other entertainments.

castanets Musical instrument consisting of two wooden shells that make a clicking noise.

cemetery Place where the dead are buried.

checkers Game played using counters on a checkerboard.

coffin Box of wood or stone inside which a dead body is buried.

duel Pre-arranged fight between two people, usually with fixed rules.

embalming Preparing a dead body for burial, using ointments, oils, and resin to preserve a lifelike appearance.

falcon Fast-flying bird of prey, like a small eagle with long, curving wings.

famine A time of hunger and starvation, usually caused by crop failure or drought.

fertile Able to grow crops or (in a human) able to have children.

festival Holiday in honor of a god, when people feast, dance, make music, and parade through the streets.

flail Wooden bar attached to a handle, used for threshing corn.

Great Pyramid Largest of the pyramids, built for the pharaoh Khufu (Cheops) at Giza near modern Cairo.

hawk Bird of prey; a kind of falcon.

hieroglyph Greek word for Egyptian picture-writing. Each hieroglyph stands for a letter, word, or idea and sometimes is a picture of what it represents.

inscribe To write or make a mark, particularly in stone.

jackal Wild dog that looks like a small wolf.

limestone A kind of rock.

ma'at Divine order; the balancing force, according to the ancient Egyptians.

mascot Animal, badge, or other object that is supposed to bring good luck.

monument Statue, tomb, or other object built to preserve the memory of a person or god.

mummy Preserved body of a dead person or an animal.

natron Mixture of salt, sodium carbonate, and sodium bicarbonate; the Egyptians used it to preserve a dead body.

papyrus A reed grown beside the river Nile; it was cut into strips, dried, and glued into layers to make a kind of paper.

patron God or person who protects or pays another for his services.

pharaoh A king in Egypt.

phases of the moon Changes in the moon's shape as more or less of its surface is lit by the sun.

pilgrim Person who travels to visit a holy place.

plague Outbreak of infectious disease that kills many people.

priest Person in charge of religious practices, leading worship, and looking after a temple and the temple god.

pyramid Huge stone building in a triangular shape, with a tomb-chamber, other rooms, and passageways inside.

resin Sticky substance that comes from the sap of pine trees and other plants.

rite Religious ceremony or a prayer to a god.

ritual Way of performing a religious ceremony or rite.

sacred Holy or set apart.

sacrifice Killing an animal and presenting it as an offering to a god.

sanctuary The holiest part of a temple, or any holy place.

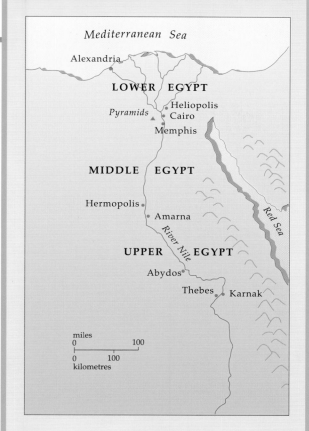

Egypt was two separate countries until around 3100 B.C. when Upper Egypt (south of Memphis) conquered Lower Egypt (north of Memphis).

OTHER EGYPTIAN GODS

ANAT Warrior and cow goddess who was a daughter of Re and wife of Thoth

ASTARTE Warrior goddess who rode on a horse, carrying weapons

HAPI Son of Horus; god of the Nile

HEKET Frog goddess of fertility and of childbirth

KHNUM Ram god from Elephantine

MIN or **MENU** Protector of crops

MONT Hawk-headed sun and warrior god

MUT Sky and cow goddess; wife of Amon

NEKHEBET Vulture goddess of Upper Egypt

SEKHMET Lion-headed goddess sent to slaughter rebellious people and criminals

SELQUET Scorpion goddess who protected women in childbirth and bodies during burial

TAWERET Hippopotamus goddess of childbirth

WADJET Cobra goddess of Lower Egypt

---

sarcophagus Stone coffin.

scarab Beetle that feeds on dung; it rolls the dung into a ball and pushes it home to feed its young. Scarabs were sacred in Egypt and often shown in jewel form.

scavenge To feed on dead bodies or food thrown away by others.

scorpion Desert animal related to spiders that has a sting in its tail.

scribe Person who writes documents.

sculptor Person who carves stone statues or makes similar works of art from clay or other materials.

serpent Another word for a snake; snakes such as cobras were common in Egypt.

shepherd's crook Staff with a curved top used by shepherds for catching sheep.

shrine A place or chamber where an image of a god is worshipped.

sistrum Wire rattle used by Egyptians in their worship.

slave Person who is not free and has to work for a master.

smith Metalworker who forges heated metal with a hammer.

soul Part of a person that is independent of the body, believed to be supernatural. After death, people are often called souls.

stonemason Person who builds with or carves in stone.

temple Place where a god is worshipped.

treachery Betrayal by trickery or deceit.

underworld Region below the earth where the souls of the dead were believed to go.

venerate To revere or treat with reverence and respect.

vizier Important state official, particularly a counselor.

INDEX

Page numbers in *italics* refer to illustrations.

A

agriculture, god of *see* Osiris
Akhenaton, pharaoh 26-27, *27*
Akhetaton 27
Amenhotep, pharaoh 26
Ammit the Gobbler 22, *22*, 24
Amon/Amon-Re 5, 9, 26, *26-27*
    temple *27*
animals/birds, sacred 4, *4*, *14-15*, *18*,
    19, 22, *22*, 24, 26, *26-27*, 28-29,
    28-29
Anubis 5, *14-15*, 22, *22-23*
Apis, bull of Memphis *28-29*
Apophis 10, *10*
    defeating *11*
astronomy 12-13
Aton, the 5, 26, 27, *27*
Atum (Re) 4, *5*

B

Bast *9*
    festival of 9, 28
    offerings to 28, *28*
Bennu *14-15*
Bes *21*
boat, sacred *11*, *26-27*
Bubastis 9, 28
bulls, sacred *4*, *28-29*

C

canopic jars 23, *23*
cat goddess *see* Bast
cats for luck 28
cats, sacred 5, 28-29, *28*, *29*
coffins *7*, *17*, *22-23*
    Osiris's 14, *16-17*
cosmetics and jewelry 21
cow goddess *see* Hathor
craftsmen 6
creator-god 4
crocodiles, sacred *24*, 29
Crocodilopolis 29

D

darkness, battle against 10
day and night 10, 24
death/the dead 6, *15*, *19*, 22, 23
    burying *23*
    gods of *see* Anubis; Osiris
    Hathor and *20-21*
    Thoth and 25
    see also mummification
desert, fear of *19*

E

earth god *see* Geb
embalming 18, *23*

F

farming *12-13*
    harvest-time *15*
    taxation *25*
festivals 8-9, 20
    of Amon-Re *26-27*
    most popular 9
funeral rites 22, *22-23*, 27

G

Geb 4, 5, *5*, 12, 13, *13*
gods:
    birth of 4
    drinking to 9
    Egypt's national god 26
    family 4, *5*
    food of 20, *20*
    see also individual gods
government officials 6, *6*

H

harp *21*
Hathor 5, 9, 20, *20-21*
hawks and falcons *10-11*, *19*, 28
hieroglyphics *4*, 24, *24-25*
home life *16-17*, 21
    god of *see* Bes
    goddess of *see* Isis
Horus 5, *5*, *13*, *16*, *17*, 18, *18*, *19*
    fight with Seth 19, 20, 24
    temple of *8-9*

I

ibis *24*, 29, *29*
Isis 4, 5, *5*, 13, 16-17, *16-17* 18, 19, 20
    finding out Re's name 16

L

law and order 6
    goddess of *see* Ma'at
learning, god of *see* Thoth
"Lord of Holy Words" 24
"Lord of the Mummy Wrappings" 22

M

Ma'at 6
marriage/marriages:
    Nut and Geb 12
    Osiris and Isis 14
    pharaohs 12
mummies/mummification *7*, *7*, 22, 23,
    23
    pets 28, 29, *29*
music/musical instruments 9, *21*

N

Nefertiti 27
Nephthys 4, 5, *5*, 13
Nile, River 4, *4*, 10
    floods *12-13*, 15
Nun 4
Nut 4, 5, *5*, 12-13, *12-13*
    children of 13

O

Osiris 4, 5, *5*, 9, 13, 14-15, *14-15*, *17*
    judgment of *19*, 22
    murder of 14, 15, *16-17*, 18

P

papyrus 25
pharaohs 6
    ancestor of 13
    burial chambers *6-7*
    regalia 14
priests 6, 8, *8-9*
    and Amon-Re 26, *26*
    Apophis ritual 11, *11*
    see also funeral rites

professionals, 6, 25, *25*
Ptah *6*, 28
pyramids *6-7*, *7*, 11

R

Ra *see* Re
Re 5, *5*, 9, 10, *10-11*, 12, 24
    and Nut's children 13
    secret name 16

S

scribes 25, *25*
"secret god" 26
serpents:
    enemy of Re *see* Apophis
    flame-spitting *see* ureaus
Seth 4, *5*, 13, *18*, 18-19, 20
    murder of brother 14, 15, 16-17, 18
shrines, sacred 8, *8-9*
Shu 4, 5, *5*, 12, 13
sistrum 21
sky goddess *see* Nut
sky watching *12-13*
Sobek 29, *29*
sun god *see* Amon/Amon-Re; Aton;
    Atum; Re

T

Tefnut 4, 5, *5*, 12
temple dancers/singers 8
temples 8, *8-9*, 27
    animals in 28, *28-29*
Thebes 26
Thoth 5, 24, *24*
    challenge to the moon 13
    offerings to 29
time, ruler of *see* Thoth
Tutankhamon 27, *27*

U

underworld, god of *see* Osiris
uraeus *12*

W

wisdom, god of *see* Thoth
world, rulers of *see* Geb; Shu
writing, invention of 24
    see also hieroglyphics